# *Sharpen Your*

# Business Letter

# *Writing Skills*

Titles in the **Sharpen Your Writing Skills** series:

Sharpen Your Writing Skills

# Sharpen Your
# Business Letter
## Writing Skills

Jennifer Rozines Roy
Sherri Mabry Gordon

**Enslow Publishers, Inc.**
40 Industrial Road
Box 398
Berkeley Heights, NJ 07922
USA

http://www.enslow.com

MAY 3 1 2012

Original edition published as *You Can Write A Business Letter* in 2003.

**Library of Congress Cataloging-in-Publication Data**

Roy, Jennifer Rozines, 1967–
    Sharpen Your Business Letter Writing Skills / Jennifer Rozines Roy and Sherri Mabry Gordon.
    p. cm. — (Sharpen your writing skills)
    Includes index.
    Summary: "Learn how to write a business letter and other kinds of business writing, the writing steps you need to follow, and the importance of rewriting and proofreading"— Provided by publisher.
    ISBN 978-0-7660-3972-8
    1. Commercial correspondence—Juvenile literature. I. Gordon, Sherri Mabry. II. Title.
    HF5721.R688 2012
    651.7'5—dc22
    2011008167

Paperback ISBN 978-1-59845-377-5

Printed in China

052011 Leo Paper Group, Heshan City, Guangdong, China

10 9 8 7 6 5 4 3 2 1

**To Our Readers:** We have done our best to make sure all Internet addresses in this book were active and appropriate when we went to press. However, the author and the publisher have no control over and assume no liability for the material available on those Internet sites or on other Web sites they may link to. Any comments or suggestions can be sent by e-mail to comments@enslow.com or to the address on the back cover.

**Illustration Credits:** Enslow Publishers, Inc.

**Cover Illustration:** Shutterstock.com

# Table of Contents

# Chapter One

# Business Writing— You Can Do It!

**Y**ou have probably been asked at least once in your life: "What do you want to do when you grow up?" While you may not know for sure what your dream job is, you probably have a good idea of what types of things interest you.

Maybe you really like animals and want to be a veterinarian someday. Perhaps you like solving mysteries and see yourself as a detective. If you really enjoy math, you might be an engineer. Or if you love small children, you could be a kindergarten teacher. Whatever career you choose, you will need to use business writing.

For example, a veterinarian might have to write a memo (short note) to other employees with instructions on how to care for the animals. A detective might

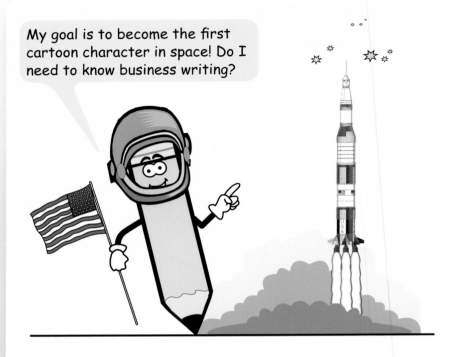

My goal is to become the first cartoon character in space! Do I need to know business writing?

need to write a business letter to the police commissioner about a case. Engineers often write business proposals to get new projects. And teachers write reports on their students' progress.

But wait. You are not an adult. You don't have a career yet. You may be asking, "Why do I need to know business writing?" The truth is, everyone has a use for business writing.

Business writing is needed to find an after-school or summer job. Suppose you want to work in that really cool toy store at the mall. Or perhaps you would like a job at a local eatery or at a childcare center.

You will need to use business writing to help you fill out the application and perhaps write a resume or cover letter to get that job. You will also need business writing skills to help you apply to college. And if you want to communicate with a business or organization, you will have to write a business letter.

## What Is Business Writing?

Business writing is the way companies and businesspeople provide information to individuals and groups. They use business writing to share ideas and goals and to make recommendations.

A business document is a piece of writing that gives information about a subject. Some examples of business documents are letters, memos, resumes, reports, and proposals.

**Something to remember:**
Some companies have stylebooks, or a set of guidelines for business documents. Stylebooks might include information on anything from whether a person's title is capitalized to the preferred formats for letters, memos, and reports.

When you get a job, it is a good idea to ask if the company has a stylebook before you begin writing any business documents.

## Why Is Business Writing Important?

Your success in getting that dream job—and keeping it—often depends on your ability to express yourself on paper. Whether it is developing a resume to help you get an interview, or writing memos, letters, and faxes to communicate your ideas once you have the job, business writing is important.

Writing for business gives you the chance to plan and organize your thoughts beforehand to communicate your message clearly. It gives you and others a written record of that message in case there are questions later. And the written word is often taken more seriously

Let's get down to business ... writing!

**Good business writing can:**
- ✔ Make you stand out in a crowd
- ✔ Help you get a job, raise, or promotion
- ✔ Demonstrate your ability to communicate
- ✔ Share your ideas and skills
- ✔ Influence and persuade others
- ✔ Cause action and get results

than a phone call, which can wander off track or be easily forgotten.

Good business writing also helps you stand out in the crowd and may help you move up in your job. In fact, a number of surveys indicate that managers consider writing skills one of the most important factors in getting promotions. What's more, many employers believe that strong writing skills show a person's ability to think clearly and make decisions. So let's get started!

# Chapter Two

# Types of Business Writing

You may be called on to write many kinds of business documents, including letters, memos, resumes, e-mails, applications, proposals, and reports.

## Business Letters

The business letter is one of the most common forms of business correspondence. Business letters communicate formal matters. They usually go directly to one person, although they may also be read by others afterward.

A business letter is printed on good quality paper or letterhead. Letterhead is stationery that is printed with a company's name, logo, address, telephone number, and Web site.

There are many different reasons for writing a business letter. They are used to make requests, to file official complaints, and to compliment someone on a job well done. They also accompany job applications, business reports, and proposals.

Here is a sample business letter you might receive after applying for a job:

## COOL KIDS DAY CAMP
67 High Street * Des Moines, Iowa * 44199

November 10, 2012

Ms. Amy Gonzalez
36 Highland Court
Des Moines, Iowa 44199

Dear Ms. Gonzalez:

Thank you for your interest in our camp. We enjoyed your interview and would like to offer you a position as counselor-in-training.

Orientation begins June 30th at 9:00 A.M. We will send you further details next week. We look forward to welcoming you to our camp community and expect to have a successful summer season.

Sincerely,

Adam Quinn

Adam Quinn
Personnel Director

## Characteristics of successful letters:

You will learn how to write and format business letters in Chapter 4, but here is a list of characteristics that will make your business letters stand out.

- ✔ Let the reader know within the first few sentences why he or she is reading the letter.
- ✔ Keep paragraphs brief.
- ✔ Make sure grammar, punctuation, and spelling are correct.
- ✔ Properly format the document and print it on good, quality paper.
- ✔ Make sure the letter is courteous, including a thank-you where appropriate.
- ✔ Keep the writing both sincere and to the point.
- ✔ The close of the letter indicates what the next step will be. For example, "I will call you next week to determine your interest."
- ✔ Be certain the letter contains a signature. Believe it or not, many people forget to sign their letters.

# Memorandums

A memorandum, or memo, typically is used to communicate with coworkers or employees within a company or organization. Memos are usually up to one page long and are often directed to more than one person within the organization. They are less formal than a business letter but still should be clear and well organized.

Usually, memos are short reminders and quick announcements that are sent out within an office. Here is a sample memo:

DATE:          December 9, 2012
TO:            Ann O'Leary, Principal
FROM:          Dennis Richardson, Cafeteria Manager
SUBJECT:       NEW FUN MENU

(Note: Instead of "SUBJECT," some businesspeople type "RE:" (for "regarding.")

As you requested, the cafeteria staff has developed a new menu that we believe the students will be excited about.

First, in addition to our daily specials, gourmet pizza will be available every day. We also have created a sundae bar that will be open on Fridays. In addition, we will experiment with a variety of food stations offering main dishes from a particular type of cuisine, such as Mexican or Chinese.

Following your approval, we will implement these changes after the holiday break. If you have questions, please contact me at 555–1256. Otherwise, I look forward to receiving your feedback by the end of the week.

## Resumes

A resume is a summary of your work experience, education, and other related activities such as internships and volunteer efforts. It can also include information about honors you have received and organizations or activities you are involved in. Resumes are used when you apply for a job and are usually sent with a cover letter that introduces you and tells what type of position you are looking for. It is recommended that resumes be kept to one page unless you have a lot of work experience to list.

## E-mail

Electronic mail, or e-mail, allows you to send and receive letters, memos, and other business correspondence through your personal computer and the Internet. For many businesspeople, e-mail is the main way to communicate. E-mail allows you to deliver messages in a matter of seconds, and you can send and receive messages almost anytime—no matter where you are.

Most businesspeople use e-mail when they need to reach a lot of people quickly with a fairly short message such as scheduling a meeting or announcing something new. Business e-mail is different from personal e-mail. It is more professional (no smileys or cute abbreviations) and has to do with work. E-mail is less formal than a business letter or memo but still should be well written.

## Applications and Cover Letters

Applications are documents used by organizations such as colleges and employers. They use applications to gather information to select the people they want for the job or to attend their school. The questions on applications ask for personal information as well as work experience. It is usually a good idea to include a cover letter when submitting your application.

Your cover letter can introduce you as a person who is interested in becoming an employee at a company or a student at a school. If there is an opening right away, the company may contact you immediately. They may also hold on to your application and cover letter until a spot opens up that might be right for you.

## Business Reports and Proposals

Business reports are similar to reports you may have written for school. In them, you communicate facts and findings from your research. Business proposals are a little different. They are also based on research, but they make requests or recommendations. You will learn much more about reports and proposals in Chapter 4.

## Personal Business Writing

Sometimes you will have to use business writing for a very important person—yourself! When you are at work, you may have to prepare notes and reports for upcoming meetings and phone calls you have to make. Business writing in this case helps you plan ahead. Writing down your thoughts and main points will ensure that you do not leave anything out and that you will get your message out clearly.

In addition, you may need to take notes during meetings and phone calls and when you are doing research for a report or proposal.

# Chapter Three

# Before You Write

Good business writing does not have to be difficult. In fact, with proper planning, it can be quick and easy. Taking the time to organize your thoughts will help you make sure that your business document is easy to understand and accomplishes what you want.

Before the actual writing, you should think about your main message and the points you want to address. You may need to do some research to gather information. You can use this planning step as a way to get the ideas flowing.

## Step One: Determine Your Purpose

When you are preparing to write a business letter or memo, you probably have a reason in mind already.

Maybe you are writing to a company about a problem you had with their product, or perhaps you are writing a memo to other employees at the store where you work.

Whatever your initial reasons for writing, it's always a good idea to make sure your purpose is clear. You should ask yourself, "What do I hope to accomplish?" You should be able to answer this question in one sentence. For instance: "I want to let the ABC Cola Company know that I have collected 100 pop tops and qualify for a new iPod." Or, "I want to be sure my coworkers know the new cash register rules."

Determining your purpose is important because you will keep it in mind as you write your document. Everything you put in the document should work toward achieving this goal.

## Step Two: Identify Your Audience

Now that you know why you are writing, you have to decide to whom you are writing. This step is important because it will let you know how to address the business correspondence and how formal you will need to be.

Perhaps I'm a bit too formal?

You should also consider how busy your reader is and how much time he or she will have to read your document. Finally, ask yourself, "Why would the reader care about what I have to say?" By knowing the answer to

## Choosing your style:

Style is not just about fashion—it is for writing, too. Choosing the right style is important to the success of your document. For example, if you are too formal for the situation, your reader may think you are awkward. On the other hand, if you are too informal you might appear childish or inexperienced.

To write effectively, think about how you would talk to the person or people who will be reading your document. For instance, if the reader is the manager or owner of the company, or if the reader is someone you do not know personally, a more formal tone would be the best choice. You would also use a formal style when writing a business report or proposal.

An informal style would be appropriate for a memo to people you work with, especially if you know them well. Just do not use cute language or too many exclamation points. You can be friendly while still sounding professional.

What about how it looks? The appearance of the document should fit in with the company's style. If you do not know what they prefer, use a medium type size with clear letters.

this question, you can create a document that not only states your purpose but also addresses your reader's concerns.

## Step Three: Gather Information

Once you have determined your purpose for writing and identified your audience, it is time to gather the information you need to put your document together. The information you need should answer the following six questions: who, what, when, where, why, and how.

Let's suppose for a minute you are the head lifeguard at your local pool. One day the pool manager tells you that the other lifeguards are not following pool procedures. He asks you to hold a meeting with the other lifeguards to be sure they know the rules and what will happen if they do not follow them.

As you gather information you will want to make certain you have answered all six questions if possible. (Sometimes you will not have an answer for every question.) To whom am I writing? The other lifeguards. What about? A meeting to discuss pool procedures. When? Date and time of the meeting. Where? Location of the meeting. Why? To be sure they know what the pool procedures are and the consequences for not following them. How should they come to the meeting? Prepared with pen or pencil and lifeguard handbook.

Make sure that your business document addresses each of these six areas when possible. You may find that you have more information than you need for the document, which is fine. Include only the information that meets your purpose and tells your audience what they need to know.

## Step Four: Outline

Now that you have decided what to include in your document, you can decide in what order it will appear. An outline is helpful for this. Your outline does not have to be a formal outline like what you would hand in for an English class, but it should help you get organized.

Here is a sample outline. It could be used for a written memo, an e-mail, or for a personal plan for making phone calls to other employees.

June 15, 2012
To:        All ABC Pool Lifeguards
From:      John Linden
Subject:   Pool Procedures

INTRODUCTION
- Opening sentence: There will be a meeting to discuss pool procedures on Thursday, June 22.

KEY POINTS
- State the time and place of the meeting
- Tell them how long the meeting will last
- Highlight briefly what will be discussed
- Explain why it is important that everyone attend
- Tell them what they need to bring or be prepared to contribute to the meeting

CLOSING
- Closing sentences: If you cannot attend the meeting, please make arrangements to meet with me at another time. Otherwise, I look forward to seeing all of you next Thursday.

## Chapter Four

# It's Time to Write!

Now it's time to write! Here are a few guidelines to help you get started. First, review your notes. Go over the material you have gathered and remind yourself of the important facts. Look over your outline and begin writing sentences that follow the order of the outline.

The key is to just write. Now is not the time to worry about grammar, punctuation, and sentence structure. You can take care of those details when you revise, edit, and proofread your document, which we will discuss in Chapter 6. For now, getting your thoughts on paper is the important part.

You have decided what you want to say in your document. So, let's find out how to write it. Each kind of document has its own format and rules. We will start with business letters.

## Brilliant Business Letters

A business letter can:

- request information
- give out information or news
- make a comment or complaint about a company, product or employee (Note: You should be cautious about criticizing someone. Stick to the facts. Do not be mean or use inappropriate language.)
- praise or thank someone

Regardless of the type, letters should always be direct, professional, and polite—even when you are making a complaint. Most importantly, business letters should be clear. State what you want the reader to do and provide all the information the reader needs to meet your request.

There are six parts to a business letter. These include the heading or dateline, the inside address, the salutation or greeting, the body, the complimentary close, and the signature. In addition, at the bottom of your letter, you may choose to add "cc" (showing who is getting a copy of the letter) or "Encl." (showing what is enclosed with the letter).

2495 Crescent Drive
Columbus, Ohio 43215          (heading)
November 22, 2012

Ms. Rachel Montgomery
Vice President of Operations      (inside address)
ABC Company
One International Drive
Columbus, Ohio 43215

Dear Ms. Montgomery:              (salutation)

On November 20, I purchased a package of your Scrumptious pudding cups. The label said that it contained three different flavors—chocolate, vanilla, and tapioca. However, when I opened the box, I was disappointed to find that all the pudding was tapioca. I notified Gregory Peters, the manager at the Happy Mart where I bought the pudding, and he suggested I contact you for a refund.

I have enclosed the store receipt and the pudding label. Please send me a refund of $3.49. I look forward to your reply.

Sincerely,                        (complimentary close)

*Keisha Bright*                   (signature)

Keisha Bright

cc: Gregory Peters
Encl.

## The Heading

The heading (also called the dateline or return address) includes your address and the date. It may also contain a phone number or e-mail address where you can be reached. Don't put your name in the heading, because it appears at the bottom of the page. Also be sure to spell out the month when writing the date.

## The Inside Address

The inside address includes the name of the person you are sending the letter to, the company's name, and their address. Including the person's name and address is very important because in large companies, business correspondence is sometimes sorted by machine in a mailroom. If the address is only on the envelope, no one will know to whom the letter should go. Make sure you spell all the names and titles correctly.

## The Salutation

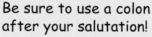

Be sure to use a colon after your salutation!

The salutation is your "hello" or greeting to the reader. Generally, it is best to use the person's last name unless you know him or her really well. For instance, write "Dear Ms. Henderson" rather than "Dear Joan." Also remember to follow your greeting with a colon, not a comma.

Use "Dear Sir or Madam:" if you do not know the name of

the person to whom you are writing (such as when you are writing to a large company to file a complaint) Or, if you know the person's title is Personnel Director, you can write "Dear Personnel Director:" if you do not know his or her name. However, it is always best to find out the name of the person to whom you are sending a letter. By writing directly to someone, your letter is less likely to be considered junk mail and end up in the trash.

## The Body

The body of the letter is the main part of your business letter. The opening paragraph is one of the most important parts of the letter. You want to make a lasting impression. Your reader should know from the first few sentences why he or she is reading your letter. Say why you are writing as clearly and quickly as possible. In later paragraphs, you can provide additional information and facts.

The ending is also an important part of the body of your letter. It is best to write an action ending, or a sentence in which your reader knows what comes next. An example of an action ending would be: "I look forward to receiving your payment" or "I will contact you in two weeks to determine your interest in meeting with me." Both sentences describe the expected action.

Finally, you should thank your reader before ending your letter—even if your letter is a complaint. For example, your final sentences might read: "Thank you for your time and consideration. I look forward to hearing from you."

## The Complimentary Close

The complimentary close is the word or phrase before your signature. It is followed by a comma. The most widely accepted complimentary close is "Sincerely." However, other acceptable closings are "Best regards" and "Yours truly." Do not use more informal closings such as "Love" and "Fondly" in business correspondence. Capitalize the first word of the closing but not the second.

## The Signature

After typing the complimentary close, move down four spaces and type your name. If you are working for a company, type your title below your name. If your letter is not written on behalf of a company, just type your name. Sign your full name in blue or black ink in the space between the complimentary close and your typed name. Remember to sign your letter neatly and legibly before sending it out.

## Carbon Copy or "cc"

When you type "cc" (which stands for "carbon copy") at the bottom of your business letter, you are letting the reader know that you sent a copy of the letter to another person. For example, if "cc: Peter Jones" appears at the bottom of your letter, the reader will know that Peter Jones received a copy of the letter as well. Also, Peter Jones will know that the letter was not written to him directly, that it is only a copy of a letter you sent to someone else.

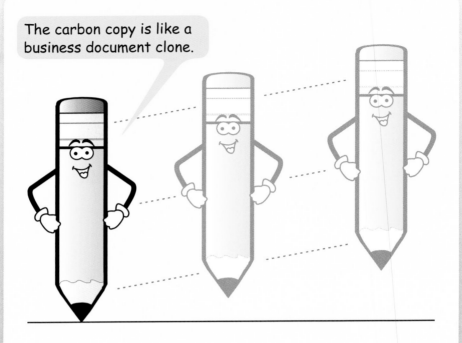

The carbon copy is like a business document clone.

## Enclosure

Enclosure (or "Encl." as it is written on the business letter) means that another document was sent with your letter. When you write a cover letter for a resume, job application, college application, or business report, you should type "Encl." at the bottom of your letter. By doing so, you let your reader know that there should be something else besides the letter inside the envelope. Before mailing your business letter, check to be sure you have enclosed your document.

## Awesome Application Letters

Although business letters such as those that request information are the kind you will write most often, letters in which you apply for a job or to a college are likely to be among the most important ones you write.

Your application letter should answer the following questions:

- What position are you applying for?
- Where did you hear about the job? (e.g., from a friend currently employed there or from an advertisement)
- Why are you interested in working for them?
- What qualifications, training, education, or work experience do you have?

**Tips for typing business letters:**

✔ Set your margins anywhere from 1 inch to 1½ inches all around.

✔ Use a colon (:) after the salutation.

✔ Use single spacing, but double space between paragraphs.

✔ Do not indent your paragraphs.

✔ Leave four spaces between the complimentary close and your name.

✔ Sign your name in ink between the complimentary close and your typed name.

✔ Keep your letter to one page.

Be confident in your letter, but be careful not to brag. One great way to show your interest is to write a sentence or two that lets the employer know you have knowledge about their company. For example, you might say:

I know from your marketing materials that you take pride in the quality of your photographs and use the latest technology to develop them. The photography courses I have taken have given me the skills to be a good photo assistant at Foto Place.

Ideally, your application letter will get you a job interview. If it does, be sure to write a brief thank you letter in business letter format after your interview takes place. Address it to the interviewers and thank them for the opportunity to meet them. Also let them know again that you are enthusiastic about working for that company.

## Marvelous Memos

A memorandum, or a memo, is a document for communicating inside a business. With memos, your audience members are employees within a company. Memos are used to communicate short reminders, quick announcements, or small pieces of information.

The opening of a memo has no salutation or inside address. Instead, it has sender-receiver information in the upper left-hand corner of the page. This information includes:

- the date
- the person you are sending it to, his/her title

- your name, your title
- the subject of your memo

Here is an example of the sender-receiver information:

| | |
|---|---|
| DATE: | September 14, 2012 |
| TO: | Stephen Chan, Principal |
| FROM: | Elizabeth Richardson<br>Senior Class President<br>Room 16<br>erichardson@abc-school.com |
| SUBJECT: | SENIOR CLASS TRIP |

It is a good idea to put in your address, telephone number, and e-mail address even to people you communicate with regularly. Including your contact information saves the other person from having to look up your telephone number or e-mail address if he or she would like to respond to your memo.

The end of your memo should contain a wrap-up sentence or paragraph. An example might be: "If you have any questions or concerns, contact me at 555–1133."

## Excellent E-mail

To create and send an e-mail message, both you and the person to whom you are writing need to have e-mail. In other words, you each need the computer software that allows you to communicate with other computers and an account with an online service provider like Yahoo or with an Internet service provider (ISP) like MSN.

In the business world, e-mail is fast and convenient and can save money. For example, e-mail messages can be sent to another country more easily and cheaply than a letter. What's more, it is a great tool for reaching a lot of readers all at one time, such as all of the employees at a company. Usually business e-mail messages are used for setting up meetings and relaying quick information or facts.

When writing an e-mail message for business, remember to be professional and courteous at all times. The rules for spelling, grammar, and punctuation also apply. You should keep your messages short and to the point. People today get a lot of e-mail messages

"You've got business mail!"

and do not always have time to read a long message. Do not use e-mail for personal reasons on the job. Do not e-mail your friends just to chat. Be professional.

Finally, think before you click "Send." Once you click it is often too late to get your message back. So be sure you are sending the message you want to send before you press the button. Also keep in mind that your e-mail message can be forwarded easily to other people, so do not say anything private in your e-mail message.

E-mail messages are very much like memos. The difference is that the e-mail software already provides the "To," "From," and "Subject" lines. All you have to do is fill in the blanks. Also, the date and time of message are added automatically and a space is provided for the message itself.

All e-mail software even provides sections to carbon copy (cc) or blind carbon copy (bcc) another person. This means that you can send people other than the intended reader a copy of your message. If their name appears in the "cc" section, they will know that the message was not written to them directly, that it is only a copy of a message you sent to someone else.

If you use the "bcc" section, the person to whom you wrote the message does not know that you sent someone else a copy. That is why it is called a blind carbon copy. Businesspeople often use the "bcc" option to let their supervisor or manager know about e-mail messages sent to other people.

Finally, remember to "sign" your e-mail by including your name at the end of the message. And, if appropriate, use a closing remark such as "Sincerely"

"Best regards." You should also include your telephone number in case the person wants to call you rather than respond electronically.

If you need to send an attachment with your message, be sure your reader or readers have the same software you have so they can open and read the attachments. It's always best to check beforehand to make sure the company accepts attachments and can open them.

## Resumes That Rule

A resume is a one- to two-page paper that will help you get a job. Think of it as putting together a written picture of yourself. You want your resume to show what skills and experience you have.

There are many accepted ways a resume can look. Choose a format that best shows off your background, experience, and education. There are a number of resume "how-to" books that can show you different formats. But do not try to be too creative and make your resume too hard to read.

**Something to remember:**
Sometimes, e-mail messages are not delivered because of a problem with the person's e-mail address or with the network. If your message is important, you can adjust the settings of your e-mail program to let you know when a message is received.

Here is one format people often use. It contains the following parts: the heading, career objective, education, experience, and references.

---

### Sarah E. Martin
36 Highland Court
Des Moines, Iowa 44199
smartin@nmz.com

**CAREER OBJECTIVE**   To obtain a daycare position.

**EDUCATION**

College Prep, Eastmoor High School,
Des Moines, Iowa, 2004
GPA: 3.75/4.0, National Honor Society

**EXPERIENCE**

*October 2009—Present*

**Mother's Helper, The Smith Family**
**Des Moines, Iowa**
- Plan after-school activities for three children, two days a week
- Assist mother of household with duties such as serving dinner, baths, and other daily activities

*June 2009—July 2009*

**Camp Counselor, Lakeside Youth Camp**
**Lakeside, Michigan**
- Coordinated daily schedule for ten 7- to 9-year-old campers
- Created daily craft projects for campers
- Led daily story time for entire camp of 100 campers

*August 2008—May 2009*

**Class President, Eastmoor High School**
**Des Moines, Iowa**
- Oversaw the development of the class homecoming float
- Planned class picnic
- Coordinated decorations and entertainment for spring dance

**REFERENCES**   Available upon request.

---

### The Heading

The heading contains all of your contact information and is located at the top of the resume. It includes your name, address, and telephone number. If you have an e-mail address you may want to include that as well.

### The Career Objective

The career objective is the job you want to have. For example, a career objective might read: "To obtain a babysitting position." Some professionals recommend not using the career objective in the resume but instead mentioning your goals in a cover letter that you send with your resume. If you choose to use a career objective, keep it short.

### The Education Section

The education section contains your educational background and training. For example, if you were applying for a manager's position at the local YMCA, you would definitely want to include your certifications from the Red Cross.

You may want to include your grade point average (GPA) in this section. If you have a high GPA, by all means include it. If you do not have a very good GPA, leave it off.

### The Experience Section

The experience section is where you list all your related experience, starting with the most recent. This information could include your work experience, your internships, and your volunteer work. If this is your first job, write down any skills or hobbies that may help you in this job.

## The References Section

References are people you know who you believe would say positive things about you. Employers often contact your references before they offer you a job.

Your references can be former employers, teachers, or other adults who know you well. Usually references are not personal friends or members of your

**Resume tips:**

1. Use powerful action verbs when you are describing your job duties. Some examples would be *coordinated*, *managed*, and *created*.

2. Use the proper verb tenses. If you still are performing the duties, use present tense, such as *teach* and *supervise*. For responsibilities that you are no longer handling, use past tense—*taught* and *supervised*.

3. Proofread your resume very carefully and be sure there are no mistakes. Almost all employers consider mistakes in resumes unacceptable.

4. Never staple anything to your resume. Put your cover letter on top of the resume and attach with a paper clip.

5. If you get an interview, be sure to bring additional copies of your resume in case more are needed.

family. Be sure to ask permission of the people you plan to list as references and thank them afterward.

Most resumes simply state at the bottom: "References available upon request." The person reading your resume will ask for the names and the telephone numbers of your references if they need them.

## Reports That Rock

In school you may have already written reports on a variety of subjects. In business, a report is much like the reports you write in school. Reports show research and findings. For example, if a company was considering a new environmental program, the person writing the report might research companies that already have such a program. The report would include his or her findings. This information might tell how well the program works, whether or not employees like the program, and what types of problems they have with the program.

When you write a report, present your information in a clear, straightforward style. Tell where you got your facts and give credit to the sources of your information.

A business report should be well organized and readable. The text of the report should be single spaced with double spacing between paragraphs. As in other business documents, your paragraphs should not be indented. Finally, the pages of the report should be numbered.

The parts of the report may vary depending on the subject of the report. The parts of the report may

**Reports you might write:**

✔ The effects of too many overtime hours on teenage employees

✔ Burgers vs. salads: why low-fat meals should be added to our fast food menu

✔ The best books to read to preschoolers

include a cover letter, title page, table of contents, executive summary or overview, introduction, body, recommendations, and appendix.

## The Cover Letter

The cover letter is a brief note that tells your reader that you have attached a report, what it is about, and why it was prepared. Writing a cover letter to go with your report shows common courtesy and good business communication skills. You should use a paper clip to attach your cover letter to your report.

## The Title Page

The title page lists the title of the report, the names of the readers and their titles, the author's name (your name) and title, and the date of the report. Usually, all this information is centered on the page. You should use larger, bolder type for the report title to make it stand out.

Here is one format you can use for the title page of your report:

---

# REPORT TITLE

Submitted to: Reader's Name
Reader's Job Title

By:
Your Name
Your Job Title

Date

---

## The Table of Contents

The table of contents lists the starting page for each section. It does not include the number of pages that the section takes up. The cover letter or memo and the title page do not receive page numbers, so they are not included here. Usually, all the information in the table of contents is single spaced.

## The Executive Summary or Overview

The executive summary or overview is one page long and tells the main points of the paper. By reading this section, the reader will know what he or she can expect to find in the report. Do not try to include too much information in this section.

## The Introduction

The introduction is the beginning section of the report. In this section, you set the scene for your reader. Give some background information. Also explain any important words used in the report if they are likely to be unfamiliar to your readers.

### The Body

The body of the report is the main part of the report and gives the reader specific information. For example, it explains the research and findings. This section is the longest part of the report.

### The Recommendations

The recommendations section wraps up the report. It should state again the report's purpose and its main points and give recommendations for the next steps. Recommendations are usually the only place in the report where you can write your own thoughts or opinions about the situation.

### The Appendix

Your appendix should contain any articles, tables, charts, or other material you used during your research. You may or may not need an appendix.

**Proposals you might write:**
- ✔ Requiring a first aid course for all camp staff
- ✔ Using natural, chemical-free cleaning products for better health in classrooms
- ✔ The need for a beverage machine in the main lobby

## Powerful Proposals

A proposal is slightly different from a report. A proposal *asks* for something, like permission to carry out a plan or for money to solve a problem. An example might be a proposal to build a new football stadium. The person writing the proposal would explain why a new football stadium is needed, the benefits to having a new stadium, and what it would cost.

Just like reports, proposals should be well organized and readable. The traditional proposal includes the following parts: cover letter, title page, table of contents, executive summary or overview, situation analysis, plan, timeline, evaluation, and any supplements.

The cover letter, title page, table of contents, and executive summary are the same as for the business report. Here are the other parts:

### Situation Analysis

The situation analysis is where you explain the current situation and why changes are needed.

I'm proposing less homework!

### The Plan

The plan is the meat of your proposal. You should begin by describing the proposal's purpose—the main action you are suggesting. (For example: "In light of the problems discussed regarding our existing stadium, we propose building a new stadium to replace it.") Then present your plan's goals and objectives. A goal is a statement of what you would like to see happen. (For example, "We would like a new stadium built in time for the 2011–2012 school year.") Objectives are the steps needed to meet each goal. (For example: "We would need to get permission from the town, raise money, and schedule construction.")

After you have listed your goals and objectives, you will write your recommended actions. These actions are the steps that must be taken to meet each objective. Your plan should provide the reader with all the details of your plan or program.

## The Timeline

The timeline is a list of dates that shows the reader when each of your recommended actions could take place.

## The Evaluation

The evaluation section lets the reader know how you plan to evaluate the success of your plan or program.

## The Budget

The budget tells the reader what it will cost.

Each type of business document is different. But no matter what kind of document you write, from letters to e-mails, resumes to proposals, one thing is clear: If you follow the business writing rules, you will look like a pro.

# Chapter Five

# Revising, Editing, and Proofreading

Y ou may think your business document is ready to go—but don't forget the revising, editing, and proofreading steps!

## Revising

Revising means checking your document's organization. Does your document need fixing? Read your work out loud to make sure it makes sense and has everything in the proper order. Then make your changes.

Here are some questions to ask yourself while you are revising:

1.  Does my document make sense? Is the purpose being met? Did I leave anything out?

2. Is the tone appropriate for my reader or readers?

3. Do all the sentences in each paragraph relate to the paragraph topic?

4. Does the document have an effective opening and strong conclusion?

## Editing

Editing means fine-tuning your document. In the editing stage you will add, cut out, or change words and phrases that do not work or sound right. Examine your words, sentences and paragraphs. Have you used clear, simple words? Have you kept your sentences short and to the point? Have you made the best word choices? Make any changes needed.

## Proofreading

Proofreading means making sure your business document is mistake-free. Do not rush through this step. This is the last step you take before submitting your document, and you want to be sure your writing is the best it can be. An effective document makes you look good.

To proofread, first print your document and read the paper copy. It is easier to see errors on paper than on a computer screen. Then, begin by checking the details of your work. This should include facts, figures, and names, as well as easy-to-miss details such as accurate page numbers and a table of contents that matches the wording in your document.

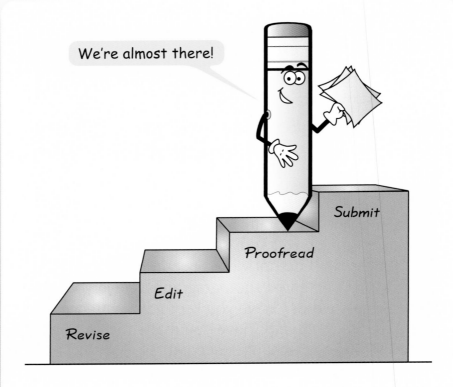

When you have finished checking the facts, look at your words and sentences. You want to be sure every word is spelled correctly and that you have all the commas in the right places. Then, when you think you are finished, look over your document one last time. Make sure it looks nice and is easy to read. It is definitely a good idea to let someone else check it over too. That person may notice something you (or your spell-checker) might have missed.

## ✓ One Final Reminder: Neatness Counts

How many times has your English teacher told the class that "neatness counts" in writing assignments?

**Proofreading checklist:**

## Check the details

1. Check all the names and titles for the correct spelling.
2. Confirm all the numbers. Are the addresses, times, and math correct?
3. Compare the dates against the calendar.
4. Check for omissions. Did you leave out any important information?

## Examine your words and sentences

5. Watch out for words that are commonly misused or misspelled.
6. Check your spelling, grammar, and punctuation. Do not rely on the computer to find all the errors.
7. Look for repeated words and small words that are easy to miss.
8. Read your document aloud. Does it make sense? If you are not sure, ask a friend or a parent to read your document.

## Look over the document one last time

9. Check your document to make sure it is formatted correctly. Are the margins correct? Are the paragraphs too long? Have you used bold and italic type to set apart the important details?
10. Study your document to see if it has a nice appearance.

These teachers are not trying to be picky. They are trying to help you form the habit of turning in professional-looking work. And, with business writing it is especially important that your documents look good.

The way someone is dressed makes an impression on you even before you meet him or her. The same is true about your business writing. The way your document looks makes an impression—good or bad—before it is even read.

If your document is not formatted properly or is messy, you are not making a good first impression. Even worse, your reader may not even bother to read it. Do not take the chance that the appearance of your business letter, memo, or report will work against you. Take time to create the neatest, most professional-looking document possible.

# Chapter Six

# Submitting Your Document

Now that you've spent all this time and effort planning, choosing the best words and format, editing, revising, and proofreading, there's one more step—choosing the best way to get your message out. Fortunately, there are a number of delivery choices available:

- regular mail
- priority mail (two to three days)
- e-mail
- fax
- interoffice mail
- overnight delivery
- handouts

## Urgent Documents and Deadlines

To decide which way to deliver your document, ask yourself how fast your document must get to the reader. Does the reader need to have your document by the end of the day, or can he or she receive it next week?

Deadlines are also important to think about. For example, you may need to send a resume to a potential employer by a certain date in order to be considered for a job. Or you may have to submit a college application by a certain date. In both cases, the deadline will play an important role in choosing your delivery option.

I'm going to make a note of the deadline, so I don't miss it!

## Document Length

The length of your document also makes a difference. Some documents are too long for some delivery choices. For example, e-mailing or faxing a lengthy document is rarely a good decision. Both e-mail messages and faxes should be kept short. Many people are irritated by long e-mail messages and long faxes. Also, with a fax machine you run the risk that not all your pages will be received.

Length also can affect the cost, especially when using regular mail. The longer a document is, the more it will weigh. And because regular mail costs are determined by weight, it might cost as much to use regular mail as priority mail.

## Making a Good Impression

Finally, think about what kind of impression you want to make. Many businesspeople are affected by the delivery option you choose. In fact, some experts say that the delivery option you choose is as important as the document itself. For example, a letter on quality paper with your actual signature makes an impression on the reader and looks much nicer than a faxed letter.

## Choosing the Best Option

After you have thought about how fast you need to get your document there, how long your document is, how it should look, and what kind of impression you want to make, then you can decide which method would be best for you. (Of course, your company may have rules about the best way to send documents, and you should follow those rules.)

## Regular Mail

Regular mail is the traditional way to send letters and packages. It is also the least expensive method. Although technology has made e-mail very popular,

### Addressing an envelope:

**1. Return Address**

The return address consists of the sender's name, street address, city or town, and zip code. It appears in the top left corner of the envelope.

**2. Mailing Address**

The mailing address is the name and address to which the letter is being sent. It always appears in the center of the envelope. There are separate lines for the name and title of the recipient; the division or department the person works in; the name of his or her company; the street address; and the city, state, and zip code.

the U.S. Postal Service is still the primary way businesspeople send their documents out—even though it is slower than other methods and delivery is not guaranteed.

## Priority Mail

Priority mail is a service offered by the U.S. Postal Service. Using this method, your document is guaranteed to reach the recipient in two to three days and sometimes sooner. Aside from e-mailing or faxing, priority mail is the least expensive way to get a document to a recipient quickly. And when mail arrives in the special blue and red priority envelope, it is likely to be opened before other mail.

## Overnight Delivery

Companies like Federal Express, (FedEx) UPS, and the U.S. Postal Service offer overnight delivery service. With this delivery option, you are guaranteed that your document will reach the reader the next weekday (weekends may not be available). You will also get a tracking number when you use one of these companies so you can always find out where your package is. The only problem is that this type of delivery can be expensive.

You would choose this delivery option when your document has to be to the reader by the next day. Because overnight delivery is very reliable and easy to track, this delivery option is also a good choice when you are sending very important documents.

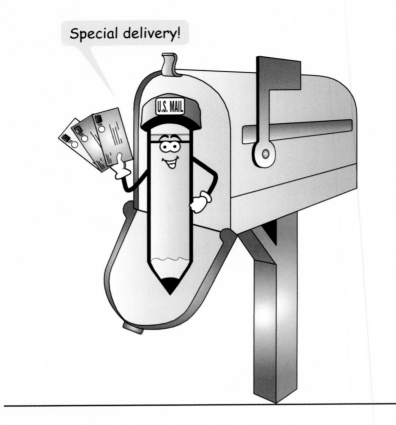

These companies also offer guaranteed second-day delivery, which is less expensive than overnight delivery. In addition, the U.S. Postal Service has such options as insured mail, certified mail, and mail with a return receipt for sending important documents. Ask at your post office for more information about these options.

### E-mail

E-mail is used when you want to get a short message to someone right away. Remember, though, to create and send an e-mail message, both you and the person to whom you are writing need to have e-mail. Usually business e-mail is used for setting up meetings and relaying quick information or facts, but you can attach a document to your message if you want–and if the other person is able to read your attachment. Keep in mind that e-mail messages can be forwarded easily to other people, so do not send confidential information through e-mail.

### Faxes

Faxes are also used to get short messages to people right away when an original copy is not necessary. Using a fax machine is useful because your document gets there quickly, it is inexpensive, and many people can be faxed at one time. For example, you might fax your reservation for an upcoming sports banquet or send a fax to confirm a telephone order. Because faxes can sometimes be unreliable, some people may fax a copy and then send a paper copy by regular mail to be sure the reader gets the document. (Like e-mails, faxes should not be used for information you want to keep private.)

### Interoffice Mail

When you have a job, you may find that interoffice mail, or mail that is sent within the office in special envelopes, is the best way to send information to your coworkers. Interoffice mail goes only to people who work for the same company, so you cannot use it if you need to send something to a person outside of the company.

Maybe someday I'll even own the company!

THE BOSS

## Handouts

If you work in a small or informal office, you may give out the documents to each person yourself.

## You Did It!

Your document has been prepared, written, and sent. Congratulations! Good business writing is important for getting a job and performing well on the job. A good business writer is a valuable employee. By following the guidance in this book, you can confidently say, "Business writing? I can do it!"

# Glossary

**application**—Document used by organizations such as colleges and employers to gather information.

**business letters**—Letters businesspeople write to communicate news and information. Business letters are more personal and formal than other forms of business communication.

**business proposals**—Documents used to make recommendations or requests based on facts and findings.

**business reports**—Documents used to communicate facts and findings.

**business writing**—Writing that companies and businesspeople use to provide information to individuals and groups. Business writing is used to share ideas and goals and to make recommendations.

**cc: (carbon copy)**—Typed at the bottom of a letter to let the addressee know that the letter is also going to another person.

**complimentary close**—In a letter, the word or phrase just before the signature, such as "Sincerely" or "Very truly yours."

**cover letter**—A letter that accompanies another document, such as a report or resume.

**document**—A piece of writing that gives information about a subject. Some examples of business documents are letters, memos, and reports.

**editing**—The process of improving a business document by adding, deleting, or changing words and phrases.

**e-mail (electronic mail)**—A computer capability that allows people to send and receive letters, memos, and other business documents through their personal computer and the Internet.

**Encl.**—Typed at the bottom of a letter to let the addressee know that another document is enclosed with the letter.

**executive summary**—A one-page overview that gives the main points of a report.

**fax**—Short for facsimile. A method of sending documents over phone lines.

**letterhead**—Stationery that has been preprinted with a company's name, logo, address, telephone number, and Web site.

**memorandum**—Often called a memo, this is a document used to communicate with coworkers or employees within a company or organization.

**proofreading**—The process of making sure your document is mistake-free.

**references**—People whose names you list for prospective employers to contact about you.

**resume**—One- to two-page summary of education, work experience, and other related activities such as internships and volunteer projects.

**revising**—The process of checking a document's organization.

**salutation**—The opening phrase of a letter, normally beginning with "Dear" followed by the addressee's name.

**stylebook**—A set of guidelines describing a company's preferences for business documents.

# Further Reading

Orr, Tamra. *Extraordinary Essays*. New York: Franklin Watts, 2005.

Yate, Martin John. *Cover Letters That Knock 'Em Dead*. Massachusettes: Adams Media Corporation, 2008.

Yate, Martin John. *Resumes That Knock 'Em Dead*. Massachusettes: Adams Media Corporation, 2008.

# Internet Addresses

**The Young Authors' Workshop**
<http://www.planet.eon.net/~bplaroch/>

**About.com**
<http://www.about.com>

**Donna Shaw's Web site**
<http://www.into.us.com/oregonstate.html>

# Index